THE LANGUAGE OF LOVE

THE LANGUAGE OF LOVE

ecstatic poems in the Sufi tradition

RAY BUCHANAN

Snake Mountain Press
Lynchburg, Virginia

SNAKE
MOUNTAIN
PRESS

Snake Mountain Press
2316 Heronhill Place
Lynchburg, VA 24503

Special discounts for bulk purchases are available. Contact publisher for more information

Cover Design: Ray Buchanan

Library of Congress Cataloging-in-Publication Data
Buchanan, Ray
A Love Note from God/Ray Buchanan
ISBN – 13: 9780988913035
ISBN 10: 0988913038
Library of Congress Control Number: 2016918302
Snake Mountain Press, Zionville, NORTH CAROLINA

This small volume is humbly dedicated to all those seeking the joy unspeakable that is so freely given. May all of us open ourselves to the Great Lover's presence, drink deeply of the sweet ecstasy he pours out for all, and finally, dance our way into his heart

Every book, regardless of size, is the product of countless layers of influence, both great and small. I lift up only three. I owe an inexpressible debt of gratitude to Chaplain Vernon Berg, USN Ret., Dr. James Collier and Dr. Jerry Shinn. All three opened new worlds to me.

INTRODUCTION

We live in a culture consistently seeking out the practical and the profitable. We are taught from an early age to live with work, to be pragmatic, to make plans, to set goals and develop strategies. And none of this is necessarily bad.

But, there is a real sense in which we are aesthetically stunted. Appreciation is lacking for art in general, and especially language arts such as poetry. Poetry is under-valued, and is most often shoved aside as of little or no worth.

I assume the reason for this comes from the fact that most Americans look upon all works of imagination as suspect, but from wherever this unambiguous distaste, and even fear of poetry arises, the result is to effectively quarantine enormous amounts of explosively powerful spiritual thought and insight.

My desire is to address this issue by offering these poems for the nourishment of both mind and spirit. *The Language of Love* is a collection of mystical poetry that could be called love poems from God.

Such mystical poetry is not new. Mystical and ecstatic poetry expressing our deep hunger for connection with the divine is a tradition centuries old.

Some poets approach their union with the divine like my personal favorite, Shams-ud-din-Muhammad Hafiz. He has a twinkle in his eye, a grin on his face, and is quick to take every possible opportunity to laugh out loud at the ridiculous nature of so much of organized religion. Hafiz loves to shock, jab, pinch and poke us into a new sensitivity of the divine. But, underneath everything he writes is his plea to enjoy oneness with the Creator.

Some, like Mirabai, give voice to a plaintive, and at times even painful, longing to be closer to the One they love. Others, like John of the Cross, go into great detail of the struggle and suffering of being separated from God.

The poetic style of each writer reflects their contemporary context, but within every poem there is the same hunger for a closer relationship with the Other. This is always the constant in such ecstatic poetry. Every poem reflects the writer's intense longing for closeness to God, by whatever name He or She is known.

In the Christian New Testament there is a passage in the First Letter of Peter where the writer tells his readers that even though they have not seen the Christ, and do not see Him right now, they still love Christ and believe in Him, and because of their love and belief in Him they rejoice with "joy unspeakable and full of glory."

The Language of Love gives voice to this universal "joy unspeakable." The poems that follow are my invitation for each of you to hear the sacred invitation and join the party.

All creation is aflame with the glorious presence of God. My prayer is that these poems will help in a small way to reveal the truth of God's deep love for us, her eternal desire for union with us, and his unwillingness to ever let us go. In the end, however, the choice is ours. Hafiz (Shams-ud-din Muhammad Hafiz), puts it this way.

A Divine Invitation

You have been invited to meet
The Friend.

No one can resist a Divine Invitation.

That narrows down all our choices
To just two:

We can come to God
Dressed for Dancing,

Or

Be carried on a stretcher
To God's Ward.

Hafiz was intoxicated with the magic and sublime beauty of the natural world, and it shows in all his work. He is sometimes referred to as "The Tongue of the Invisible," because so many of his poems appear to be ecstatic love songs from God. As Emerson once remarked, "Hafiz is a poet for poets."

The work of Hafiz never gets old for me. I return to the poetry of this Sufi master over and over to drink from the sacred well he has dug.

All sacred art is an attempt to open the soul to a deeper perception of life's spiritual dimension. *The Language of Love* is a humble collection of Sufi inspired poems that attempt to capture the deep yearning, the infinite tenderness, and exuberant joy of God's unending love for each of us.

The central charm of Sufi poetry is in its deep symbolism. Everything contains multiple levels of meanings.

The symbols commonly employed by the Sufi poets such as Rumi, Hafiz and other Persian poets are ones that would be most familiar to their readers. Wine (prohibited by Islam) is the symbol for divine love, and in turn, the mystical knowledge it brings. Intoxication, or being drunk, refers to ecstasy or direct knowledge of the divine.

The Beloved, the Friend, and the Tavern Keeper are all references to God, or maybe another human in whom the divine qualities are clearly reflected. Spiritual seekers and students became clowns, beggars, rogues, drunks, scoundrels and courtesans.

The tavern is the "Tavern of Ruin," a lonely place outside of town, the gathering place of the Sufis. It's away from mosques, a place where wine is served and rogues and scoundrels gather. More importantly, the tavern is the opposite of the mosque (or the church). It is a place of freedom, away from those who use religion as a means to inflate their own self-image.

The tavern goers are the lowest of the low. They're the ones that recognize their poverty. Their humility is real. They are the ones, therefore, open to genuine spirituality.

As you read these poems, my desire is that you might experience a blurring between human and divine love. The two are ever entwined and always inseparable.

In the end, all love is transformative, and is but an aspect of our love for God. And all love leads to the heart of God. If we will open ourselves to the passionate love God has for us, that love will lead us beyond ourselves and straight into his arms.

Ray Buchanan
Lynchburg, Virginia
August 2017

THE POEMS

A CELEBRATION OF LIFE

Every soul
should receive medals
for bravery.
And all of us
should drink together
in celebration
of our victory
over a harsh
and cruel world.
Let's drink,
and laugh
until even the
tavern keeper himself
gives up on
keeping the jugs
on our tables filled.
Then, when he
throws open the doors
to the wine cellars
we will dance
through the universe
with him
on our shoulders.

DANCING IN THE MOONLIGHT

Hold on to me
as we dance
in the moonlight.
Only the great lover
could throw such a party,
where the sweets
form sugar mountains
and the wine
flows without ceasing.
Here's to the one
who leads the dance!
Lift up your hearts
and let your laughter
fill the night sky.

GOD'S LAUGHTER

I think it was God's laughter
that formed the worlds
and stars we see and know.
Maybe a quiet little chuckle
is how it all began. But,
it was his knee slapping
cosmos shaking, belly laugh
that brought tears to his eyes
and each of us into his heart.

LOOK, THE MOON IS BLUSHING

I can hear the laughter of the sea
as it plays with the white sand.
A little bite here, a little lick there,
their passion is building
and the spray is beginning to fly.
No wonder the moon
is trying to hide behind the clouds.
Doesn't she know
that the two lovers
have nothing to hide?
Actually, she's the one
that has gotten them both
so turned on.

THE REAL THING

There's no need
to burn all the books
about God.
That's really
not necessary at all.
Just remember
that reading a book
about God,
even a great and
most holy book,
is like looking
at a picture
of a beautiful woman.
Why waste your time
just looking
when all the while
she is begging you
to make
wild and passionate love
to her?

GOD IS ONE

The more I travel
the more I see God
in every face.
Maybe, that is why
a smile is never
out of place,
and laughter
never needs translation.

LISTEN TO THE ROSES

The moon is full and round
and close enough tonight
to excite every flower in my garden.
Listen, and you can hear them
whispering their hopes and hungers.
All of them, from the roses
to the peonies,
all of them
want the very same thing.
They are full of lust
and can wait no longer
for the sweet taste of love.

ON THE HOUSE

The hurdy-gurdy
in the old tavern
only plays
happy tunes;
and why not?
The tavern keeper
is giving away
his best wine
for free.
It's time
for the dancing
to begin.

ANYTHING ELSE IS A WASTE OF TIME

With the freedom
of a beggar
reduced to nothing,
I want to dance
full of the joy
of having everything
that matters.
Let all who
hunger and thirst
listen and learn.
Love!
    Love!
      Love!
There is nothing else!

BOTTOMS UP!

Stop being
so incredibly dainty.
Sipping
from the jug
of God's love
is an insult.
Ecstasy is meant
to be chugged.
All of us
need to be smashed
with such joy.

GOD IS WAITING FOR YOU

On the bedside table
is a jug of pure ecstasy,
beside it, a platter
heaped high
with perfectly ripe joy.
And in the bed,
the divine lover
waits to get you
between the sheets.
Throw away your books
about God.
Now is your chance
To experience love.

EAVESDROPPING ON TWO LOVERS

Please,
not so hard.
Don't be
so rough,
I heard the sand
whisper
to the sea.
The waves'
only response
was a foaming grin,
again baring
those curling
teeth of white.
Immediately,
I watched
as the beach
exposed even more
of her
already damp breast
to the sea's
wet mouth
Only then,
Did I finally understand
the true nature
of the game.

I KNOW THE TAVERN KEEPER

Will you sing with me
as we dance together
toward the tavern door?
Listen to the music
flowing into the street!
The moon is a silver platter
full of love and promise,
and the tavern is full
of fresh sweet wine.
Sing with me
as we dance together
toward the heart of God.

LAUGHTER AMONG FRIENDS

Laughter
among friends
is like sacks of gold
among the poor.
Pour it out
until we are all
covered in it.
Let it ring out
until all the neighbors
come to investigate.
And, once they too
are covered,
open all the doors and
throw open the windows.
Fill the street
with joyous dancing.

PARTY HARDY

I hear singing in the distance
and know the party has begun.
Every morning it's the same.
The sun wakes up the birds,
who then wake the trees, who
then get the breezes blowing.
That's when the grasses and flowers
start dancing. By this time
there's just no stopping.
All nature is partying down.
You just got to love it.
The cosmic laughter says
he certainly does.

SO MUCH MORE

You want
to hold hands
with God.
That's ok –
but God wants
so much more.

You want a little kiss
on your cheek
from God.
That's ok –
but God wants
so much more.

You want
a gentle hug
from God.
That's ok –
But God wants
So much more.

God is madly
And passionately
Infatuated with you.
What God wants
is to wrap you

in his arms,
covering you
with his presence.

What God wants
is a kiss
that creates
whole new worlds.

What God wants
is to look
so deep
into your eyes
your soul will
melt for joy.
What God wants
is for you
to just let go
and allow him
to love you.

PRAY NAKED

Going into the church,
I was saddened
when my spirit
could no longer sing.
I heard no laughter.
I saw no joy.
I couldn't even hear
the voice of God.
It's obvious,
at least to me,
that we once again
need to learn
the absolute freedom
that comes when we
pray naked.

THE BAWDY BARKEEP

My friend,
the old bartender,
whispers stories
of love to me,
trying to get me aroused.
It works.
I'm hard as a rock.
And I know
I can move mountains.
He knows the passion
in my soul.
You cannot hide love.

YES! YES! YES!

It's the naked dancer
that draws closest
to the heart of God.
Why is that so surprising?
It's the naked dancer,
so freely whirling,
that has not only heard
the invitation,
but has answered,
Yes! Yes! Yes!

THE PARTY IS JUST STARTING

Hold on tighter
and I'll spin you again.
The dance has just begun.
Together, we will spin
among the stars.
Together, we will whirl
among the planets.
Yes. Hold on tighter.
The music is getting louder
and the wine has yet
to be served. Tonight
my heart is on fire
and there's no limit
on love.

WATCH THE TREES

I love it when the cedars
do their sexy dance.
The way they sway comes
straight from the heart.
They listen to the divine drums
and then just let it happen.
They mirror
the soul of God.

THE DIFFICULT
QUESTION

People ask me
why I am always
so happy.
They cannot seem
to understand
the joy that pours forth
from the depths
of my heart and soul.
When I try to explain
they will not listen.
Maybe it's because
the answer sounds
too simple.
See God in everything.
Hear him in everything.
Realize that love
powerful enough
to create the cosmos
surrounds you,
engulfs you,
penetrates you,
and calls you by name.
How can one be
so totally, so fully,

so completely loved
and not express it?
That, I think,
is the really difficult
question.

THIS MORNING

I awoke this morning
to the sound
of God laughing.
Then, I saw him
dancing among the sunbeams.
Unless I am mistaken,
I am sure I heard him
invite me to join him.

THE TAVERN KEEPER'S DELIGHT

Why do you sit
with a mouth like dust
and a throat too parched to sing?
The tavern keeper's delight
is pouring his love without measure,
without cost.
How else could we all
be singing so loudly?
We are beggars
of the Great King,
and we all need our wine
morning, noon, and night!
So, don't sit there
with a tormented mind
and burdened soul.
Drink. Drink
until you can hold no more.
Then, join us
in the singing.
We're scoundrels, one and all.

A COSMIC JIG

How difficult it is
for God to dance
in the midst
of stained glass frowns.
Doesn't anyone else
hear his booming laughter.
Get naked.
It's time to pray.
Let's all join God
in a cosmic jig.

WHEN SPIRITUALITY LEAVES A MARK

Could it be
that the true measure
of our spirituality is
the size of the love bruise
it leaves on our neck?

Maybe it's
the size of the love bruise
it paints on our brain.

It might be
the size of the love bruise
woven into our soul.

What do you think?

As for me, well,
I think
it's most likely
all three.

BETTER THAN A LOVE NOTE

I was already asleep, dreaming of love,
when a star came crashing down
through my bedroom window.
As soon as I heard the laughter
I called out her name.
No one but her could love
me that much. She has
a passionate streak that can melt
mountains, boil oceans
and lead me straight into
the kingdom of heaven.

A LITTLE SECRET

What God wants from you
is not what you think.
He's really not interested
in a lifelong struggle
for purity and sainthood.
If you really want
to make God happy,
just give him
a big ol' open-mouthed kiss.
His joy
will explode stars
in galaxies yet to be created.

THE CLOUDS ARE
READY TO BOOGIE

I can tell
that the clouds
want to dance.
You can see it
in their faces.
The great lover
has them all
excited and
laughing hysterically.
They want to play.

A LOVE NOTE FROM GOD

Thanking God,
I realize I am not alone.
Beside me,
I see the sun
and the moon
and all the myriad
of stars.
All, like me
are bowing to God
in gratitude.
Our happiness
is in realizing
just how great
the love of God
really is.
The entire cosmos
is a love note
sealed with
the divine lips.
No wonder all creation
is lost in praise
and adoration.

A SIMPLE REQUEST

God is love.
I want all of God.
I want all of love.
So, let me love you
until our ecstasy
lifts us both
into the very arms
of God.

YOU LOOK THIRSTY,
MY FRIEND

I can see from your face
that your heart is an empty bowl.
The question is,
do you really desire
to have it filled to overflowing?
The choice is yours, you know.
Your dry, parched soul
is testimony that you too
have played the fool,
listening to promises
as empty as a camel's farts.
Just a nod at the tavern keeper,
and jugs of the finest wine
will fill your bowl
with life-giving love,
enough for you, and
enough for rogues everywhere
to share.

THE LANGUAGE OF LOVE

I heard the Happy One
call my name.
Those around me
thought it was
just the buzzing
of a fly.
I winked.
And, of course,
the fly winked back.
The two of us know
God's love
surrounds us
on every side.
Neither of us
could stop laughing.

ALL OR NOTHING

The true saints
are the ones
who have bet
everything
that God is real.
Forget the odds.
With a gambler's
blind courage
They are going for broke.
It's either everything
or absolutely
nothing.
Listen to their
holy laughter.
Freedom is just
one result of saying
Yes! Yes! Yes!

DON'T BE AFRAID TO LOVE

Don't be afraid to love.
Be afraid instead
of trying to bottle up
the cosmic joy of creation.
Can you hold back
the heart of God?
So don't try. Just
let love flow.
Then you will begin
to understand why
I am always laughing.

ALL WE NEED TO DO IS TO WAKE UP

Awakening
to fruits and grains
and little pots
of wine and milk
I realize
I am being courted.
I hear the soft sounds
of your singing
and my heart
is comforted.
Even before
I can utter
a hesitant response,
the light of
all creation
fills my emptiness
and I know
the meaning of love.

COME ON, THE BAND IS PLAYING

Stop being
so very afraid
of letting go.
The arms
of the King
are around us all.
You will not fall.
Let go,
and feel the
ecstasy of love.
Then you too
will shout
and want to
join the dance.
I'll wait for you.
But, please hurry!

ALL I WANT

All I want
is to know
the heart
of the Beloved.
The rest
is simply
details.

EVERYONE KNOWS THE TUNE

I know what Hafiz means
when he warns of counterfeit pleasures.
How often have I had my moment,
only to be dragged for days
like a broken man
behind a farting camel?

But, now I want to learn.
I want to know the astonishing light
of my very own being.
I want all attachments freed
to float or fall wherever they will.

And then, I want to lead
all the singing. That's right.
I want to lead all the singing
as I give myself
to the great journey of love.

FEASTING AT LOVE'S TABLE

Like the moon,
We are most radiant,
We are most happy,
When we are full.
That's why
God's table is always free,
and the invitation
is extended to everyone.
Come eat and drink
without money
and especially
without fear.
The beloved himself
awaits to fill our cup
with sweetest ecstasy
and our plates
with purest joy.
Let the banquet begin!

FINDING OUR WAY HOME

The heart
is God's compass,
always pointing
out the true direction
of love,
always leading us
toward our home.
No matter
how far off
we wander,
we can never
be lost.
The way home
is love.

IN THE IMAGE OF GOD

How can you say
"no!"
to love?
You would dare
turn your back
on the Beloved?

We're fashioned
in love, by love,
for love, to love.

Don't you see?
Love is not
Something
We can choose
or not choose
to do. Love
is the very essence
of who we are.

LET'S HAVE A PARTY

Let's strip naked
and dance in the moonlight.
The flowers will sing for us,
the trees will all clap,
and once we are spinning
wildly enough, I know
the stars will come
and join us.

IT WORKS FOR ME

I have tried to be a saint.
It didn't work.
I made a thousand promises,
and struggled
to keep heroic vows.
It didn't work.
Now that I have quit
such foolishness
I have time
to hear God laughing.
Now, I have time
to love
and to serve him.
Now, I am happy,
and he is filled
with great joy.
Now, I am myself,
loved, accepted
and filled with
the power
of all creation.
It works for me.

LET'S ALL LAUGH TOGETHER

Look around you.
On every side
there are precious souls
searching to find
the light.
Like tiny
crushed angels
with wings far too fragile
they still struggle to fly.
Come.
Help me
set out little pots
of wine and milk
so we may all grow strong
and laugh together.
Soon we will soar
past the stars
straight
into the waiting heart
of God.

IT SEEMS TO ME

We should all be dancing.
All of us should be singing,
celebrating,
reaching out
to let all those we meet
know how glorious it feels
to be given the freedom
to be ourselves. Surely
we should be ecstatic.
Why then aren't we all
dancing?

LISTEN CLOSELY

Dry and brown,
the Holy Land
spreads out
beneath me.
Hills, mountains,
valleys and wadis
all lift up
their individual
poems of praise.
I hear the echoes,
even at
seven thousand
feet.

LET THE PARADE BEGIN

I have begun listening to the poet.
Yes, I know it is dangerous,
but the rewards are great
and his wine is sweet and pure.

Now, I am starting to see
the astonishing light.
Yes, it really is within all of us,
and that means, yes, it means
we are all free.

Slowly, I am beginning to understand.
Within me is the beautiful
Ancient Warrior basking
in the sublime glory
of God's everlasting love.

I am finally ready to join hands
with the one who comforts my soul.
It is time for eternity's parade to start.
The joy of my heart
will set the tempo.

A HOLY MOMENT

Wouldn't you like to be free
like David
dancing naked before the Lord?
I know he could hear
God's laughter.
He could also probably see
the tears of joy
streaking his God's face.
Just thinking about it
makes me tremble.
A king wildly dancing
for his King.
Some things are too beautiful
to even speak aloud.

THAT YOUR JOY MAY BE FULL

When I say
I want to kiss you,
please don't refuse me.
I want your heart
to be as full of God
as mine.

NOW YOU KNOW

To know God
is to understand
we are free to say a holy Yes!
To all creation.
Knowing God
is to understand
there is no word
for No in God's heart.
Now you know
why I cannot keep myself
from laughing.

LOOKING FOR LOVE

The wind has settled down,
but the cedars still sway
ever so sensually in the breeze,
offering themselves
to the lips of the sky.
No wonder the stars
shine so brightly tonight.

THE DIVINE LOVER

Why are you
so afraid?
God
is not a rapist.
He is,
however,
the most
incredibly sensitive,
deeply amorous,
well endowed
lover of all creation.
And all he wants
is to give you
joy unspeakable.
Just what exactly
are you waiting for?

THE GOOD NEWS

The good news is love.
God is love. God loves us.
God wants us
to love each other.
God wants us
to share the good news.
So, why aren't you
dancing for joy?
Why do you still
have such a big frown?
Haven't you heard
a thing I've said?
God loves us!
The good news is love.

WAITING ON THE BELOVED

My heart is thirsty
for the pure sweet wine
that only the Beloved
can provide.
My heart is hungry
for the figs and pots of honey
that only comes
from His hand.
Tonight I need
the Beloved to feed me
as only He can.
When He comes
I know I will be filled.

THE PARTY IS JUST STARTING

Hold on tighter
and I'll spin you again.
The dance has just begun.
Together, we will spin
among the stars.
Together, we will whirl
among the planets.
Yes. Hold on tighter.
The music is getting louder
and the wine has yet
to be served. Tonight
my heart is on fire
and there's no limit
on love.

THE PERFECT PATH

I finally decided
to give up my struggle
to find the perfect path
to the heart of God.
That's when I heard
his soft laughter. There
was relief in his voice
as he whispered "finally."
Since then, my heart
overflows with praise
and all creation
soaks me with the perfume
of my beloved.
I am the path.

THE SECRETS OF LOVE

My tavern keeper tells me secrets
that no one else could know.
He drinks like a fish, smells like a goat,
and laughs like a braying ass.
But, the secrets he knows
are better than the wine
that he serves me for free.
He knows the ways of love.
I think he may have even
written the book. One day,
when I think he is drunk enough,
I'm going to ask him.
I can already hear
the braying of his laughter.

GOD'S CLASSROOM

I now realize
that all of creation
is God's divine classroom.
Each of us
has our own place,
and each of us
proceeds at our own pace.
But, the very best part
is that each of us
is the teacher's pet.

THE MOON IS FULL

Bull Frogs set the beat
with crickets sawing away
to keep up the tempo.
A single owl
adds the
occasional
note of
syncopation,
and the music of the night
just keeps getting better
The forest floor
is now packed
to overflowing
with creatures
great and small,
all dancing
like there is no tomorrow.
I look at the Bandleader
and he just grins
and gives me a big wink.
The moon is full,
the night is young,
and the party
is just getting started.

YOUR HAPPINESS

Every time you smile
a thousand angels
break into applause.
And when you laugh,
Stars and even galaxies shake
from the standing ovation
you receive.
Now, you know
why I pray
so often
for your happiness.

TREASURE CHEST

I talked
with the friend
this morning.
And, as always,
the secrets
he shared
were better
than the fabled
chest of gold
at the rainbow's
end. And the only thing
he said was
love is the single treasure
large enough
to purchase
forgiveness.

BFF BAR & GRILL

True sustenance
cannot be purchased
like so much
beans or rice,
and there's
a vast gulf
between
staying alive
and living.

The true food,
that food
that feeds our heart,
the food we most need,
is always on tap
at the BFF Bar & Grill.
Forgiveness flows freely,
and love is on the tables
twenty-four/seven.

WATER OF LIFE

There are lands
where life
is measured, and even
defined,
by water…
or the lack of it.
This humble poet
has witnessed
precious souls
spend their days
walking miles
to scoop
battered and broken buckets
and cracked clay jugs
in foul
muddy pits
to quench a thirst
that never goes away and cannot be slaked.
Yet, the Friend
promises us
a living well,
that flows
from the heart of the universe,
a spring of love, crystal pure.

THE NAME OF THE GAME

When the moon is full,
like it is tonight,
nothing is better than
to grab a huge handful
of the sky and the earth
and revel in the vastness
of the Great Lover's heart.

When the moon is full
like it is tonight,
there are no rules
on this divine playground.
The name of the game
is love, and all of us
are the winners.

WINE AND WISDOM

My friend, the bawdy barkeep,
and I had a long discussion
as we often do, talking for hours,
allowing the wine and wisdom
flow without concern
for either time or measure.
Somewhere in the middle
of that evening's conversation
my friend pointed
his fat, stubby finger at me,
loudly belched, and asked
wouldn't it be grand
if we could make love
into a virus?
I paused for just a second,
then slowly nodded
in the affirmative
as I answered,
only if I could be the first infected.
I would want to be the carrier.
We both laughed
as we again lifted our mugs
in a mutual toast
to wine and wisdom.

HOW CAN OUR TONGUES BE STILL?

Are there any so blind
than those who refuse to see?
We live, we move,
we have our being
in this divine playground
created just for our pleasure.

If our eyes are open,
if our ears can hear,
how can our tongues be still?
Stars beyond counting sing praises
Flies by the millions buzz their thanks
for such wondrous provision.

We've been granted a playground of love
designed just for our enjoyment.
Rocks and trees, mountains and valleys,
rivers and oceans, and all living things,
both great and small, are all ours.
How can our tongues be still?

NO TRANSLATION NEEDED

There are times
when I get still enough
and become silent enough
that I can hear
exactly what that silly fly
(that can never be still),
is trying to say to me.
I have to listen intently,
and really focus
on what my little friend is saying,
but I have learned
it's definitely worth the effort.
The language of love
needs no translation.
We just need to pay
much closer attention.

A UNIVERSAL TONGUE

I've never been good
at picking up languages.
Yet, as I get older
and hopefully a little wiser,
I have begun making
a little headway in learning
the language of love.
I've discovered, for instance,
that it's a universal tongue
where actions speak
even more loudly than words,
and where conjugation
is best accomplished
with a hug and a kiss.

A LESSON FROM THE BUSH

I once watched
a tickbird
riding on the back
of an old and scarred
Cape Buffalo.
I think
it might have been
in Botswana,
although the location
isn't all that important.
What is important
is that I watched
as bird and beast
(the large and the small),
not only coexisted, but
actually proved
significantly beneficial
to one another.
This poet
humbly suggests
it's a lesson
we would all
do well to learn.

THAT FIRST KISS

The Friend
is always waiting for you,
right outside your door.
He's patient, and waiting
for that first kiss
of the morning.
Don't leave home
without it.

FOLLOW MY TRACKS

Don't wait,
until it's too late,
my friend.
Follow my tracks
across the barren wastes
of what some
name as religion.

Yes,
the sand is blistering,
the sun
saps all the moisture
from the air,
and every breath
seems like your last.

But,
believe me,
my friend.
I am waiting for you,
and the owner of the oasis
knows you
are on the way.

LET THE ROSE TEACH YOU

I see your heart
my dear friend,
squeezed so tightly shut.
And I understand.
But please, believe me.
There's really no need
to remain fearfully
wrapped within yourself.
Just sit silently
before the rose and learn.
Watch how the rose
allows the divine light
of the Creator's love
to gently pry
its promise
into a glorious
bloom of praise.

AN HONEST ANSWER

Why can so few
see the true beauty
of our brothers and sisters
with no hips?
That's the question
I posed to my good friend,
the bawdy barkeep, hoping
he was drunk enough
to give me
an honest answer.
His braying laughter
caused heads to turn,
and once
he wiped the tears
from his eyes
he answered in a whisper
only I could hear.
Don't you understand?
Everyone needs something
to look down on,
and everyone knows
that religion
teaches us
to fear the truth,
especially if it slithers.

DIVINE VOCABULARY

From a high peak
you can see for many miles
if the day is cloudless and clear.

But, there's a divine Peak
in each of our hearts
where we can see forever.

Once we scale that peak
and gaze into the Creator's heart,
we can finally understand.

It's on that lofty pinnacle
we learn the divine vocabulary,
the language of love.

FOLLOW THE SNAKE

The path
is open to all,
and the joy
we all seek
is far closer
than most
might think.
Listen to the owl.
Follow the snake.
Together, they
will lead you
into the arms
of the Great Lover.

EYES FOR YOU

The tavern keeper
sees me coming
and quickly put out
a bottle of his best.
Then, seeing you,
he pulls out
several more bottles
and glasses
for the three of us.
It's obvious
that he has eyes for you.

ZAMBEZI SUNSET

Watching
the sun set
on the Zambezi,
the river becomes
a molten gold
bridge
straight
out of Africa
into the Creator's heart.

HEIRLOOM SEEDS

My garden
is ready,
waiting for the seeds
from the Divine Garden catalog.
There's several varieties of compassion,
and a couple more
of mercy, as well.
I also ordered understanding, care
and a climbing openness.
But, the largest
space in my garden
is always saved
for the infinite varieties
of love.

LETTER OF LOVE

The Great Lover
talks with me
without the need
for words.
I hear his promises
in every breeze,
and the crickets
never allow me
to forget his passion.
All of creation
is his unending
letter of love.

THE FIRST DANCE

Wake up.
The room is full
and it's time to play.
The feast
is already spread
and the wine is waiting.
Come, my love.
God has asked you
for the first dance.

COME QUICKLY

There are secrets
revealed only
by the Great Lover.
So, come quickly,
my love.
Come quickly.
The night is alive
with ecstasy,
desire and delight.
And now, the Friend
is calling your name.
Come quickly.

GET HERE SOON

Our wine jugs
are full
and the tavern keeper
has the music blasting.
Tonight is a night
made for love,
and there are wondrous secrets
being told.
Don't miss out.
Get here soon, my friend
Get here soon.

TIME TO WORSHIP

My friend,
the tavern keeper
met me
this morning
at the tavern door.
In one hand
a full jug
of chilled honey wine,
and in the other,
a platter heaped
with fine cheeses
and crusty bread
still warm from the oven.
His beaming smile
was my invitation.
He knew
I had come to worship.

OFTEN, I FIND MYSELF ON MY KNEES

Wine is a grace,
a gift
made for worship.
But, I really
don't need its sweet ecstasy
to delight
in all the wonders
of the glorious
and totally intoxicating gift
so freely given.
Often, I find myself
on my knees
under the nearest tree.
The Friend
surrounds me
with arms big enough
to create the cosmos,
yet gentle enough
to stroke a sleeping fawn.
His love calls me
to unceasing prayer,
and to that joy
unspeakable
and full of glory.

THANK YOU, MY FRIEND

My blueberry bucket
was half full
this morning
before the circling hawk
reminded me
I was in church.
So I paused there
on my knees,
and once again
offered my praise
for love so freely given,
and my thanks
for the glories
I've too often
taken for granted,
or simply ignored.
Your presence
surrounds us, my Friend,
and your love
never lets us go.
Thank you, my Friend.
Thank you.

OUR PRAISES FILLED THE BERRY PATCH

Worship
this morning
was an unceasing
praise service.
The entire
congregation
refused
to allow the music
to stop,
And our praises
filled the
berry patch
as an unending offering
to the Great Creator.
From the June Bugs
to the bees,
everyone present
entered in.
A Mockingbird
had a haunting solo,
beautifully supported
by a duet of doves.
and all I could do
was to again whisper
thank you.

LEAVE A FEW FOR MY OTHER FRIENDS

The Friend met me
this morning
while I was in the middle
of the berry patch.

Laughing at me,
he winked
and told me
don't pick them all.

Leave a few
for my other friends.
Mockingbirds
enjoy blueberries, too.

PLAYING CHURCH

Is worship
without praise
truly worship?
Is worship
without joy
truly worship?
Is worship
without holy laughter
that brings tears
to our eyes
truly worship?
Or, could it be
just playing church?

.

ABOUT THE AUTHOR

Ray Buchanan has made ending global hunger his life's goal, founding or cofounding three different hunger organizations that have provided millions of dollars' worth of food and support to those desperately needing it.

Buchanan received his bachelor's degree from the University of North Carolina at Wilmington and his master's degree in divinity from Southeastern Baptist Theological Seminary. He was later awarded a doctorate of divinity from Shenandoah University and a doctorate in humane letters from North Carolina State. Buchanan spent four years in the US Marine Corps, serving in Japan, Okinawa, and Vietnam.

Among the awards Buchanan has been honored with for his charitable efforts are the University of North Carolina at Wilmington Alumnus of the Year Award, the Caring Institute National Caring Award, the National Association of Christians and Jews Humanitarian Award, and the North Carolina Human Rights Award.

Buchanan is an ordained elder of the United Methodist Church. He lives in Lynchburg, Virginia with his wife, JoAnna, and teaches at Lynchburg College in the Graduate Program for Nonprofit Leadership Studies.

www.ingramcontent.com/pod-product-compliance
Lightning Source LLC
Chambersburg PA
CBHW031600040426
42452CB00006B/363